This book
belongs to

_____

who is a very important person
whom God will always love.

Before I Was Me

SOPHIA
INSTITUTE PRESS

Text and Images Copyright © 2018 Frank Fraser

Printed in the United States of America.

Sophia Institute Press®
Box 5284, Manchester, NH 03108
1-800-888-9344

www.SophiaInstitute.com

Sophia Institute Press® is a registered trademark of Sophia Institute.

Library of Congress Cataloging-in-Publication Data

Names: Fraser, Frank, author.

Title: Before I was me / written and illustrated by Frank Fraser.

Description: Manchester, New Hampshire : Sophia Institute Press, 2018.

Identifiers: LCCN 2017056109 | ISBN 9781622826063 (pbk. : alk. paper)

Subjects: LCSH: Vocation—Christianity—Juvenile literature. | Creation—Juvenile literature.

Classification: LCC BV4740 .F68 2018 | DDC 248.4—dc23

LC record available at https://lccn.loc.gov/2017056109

7th Printing

Before I Was Me

written and illustrated by
Frank Fraser

SOPHIA INSTITUTE PRESS
Manchester, NH

When I was very, very new,
still growing in my mother,
I asked God,
"Who will I become?"

"Oh, my little one, I have **great plans** for you!

I have chosen you to be a very important person whom I will always love!"

God's words filled me with joy!

I was going to become a very important person! In an instant, I knew I would become...

An astronaut!

"They are very important because they are the only people who go off to work in a rocket!"

"Every morning, I will go off to work on Mars. It takes a long time to get there, so I will stop halfway for some milk and cookies."

"How will you get these cookies?" whispered God in my ear.

"I don't know — who could help me?"

"A baker," suggested God.

"Then I will become..."

A baker!
"They are very important because they make all the yummy treats everyone wants!"

I will bake day and night until the whole world knows me and my treats. I will pour and splash and mix and whip delicious ingredients that every customer loves."

"How will you get these delicious ingredients?" whispered God in my ear.

"I don't know — who could help me?"

"A farmer," suggested God.

"Then I will become..."

A farmer!

"They are very important because they grow food for hungry people around the world."

I will drive a big tractor, and water plants when they're thirsty. I will need others to help me, unless, of course, they get sick; then I will help them!"

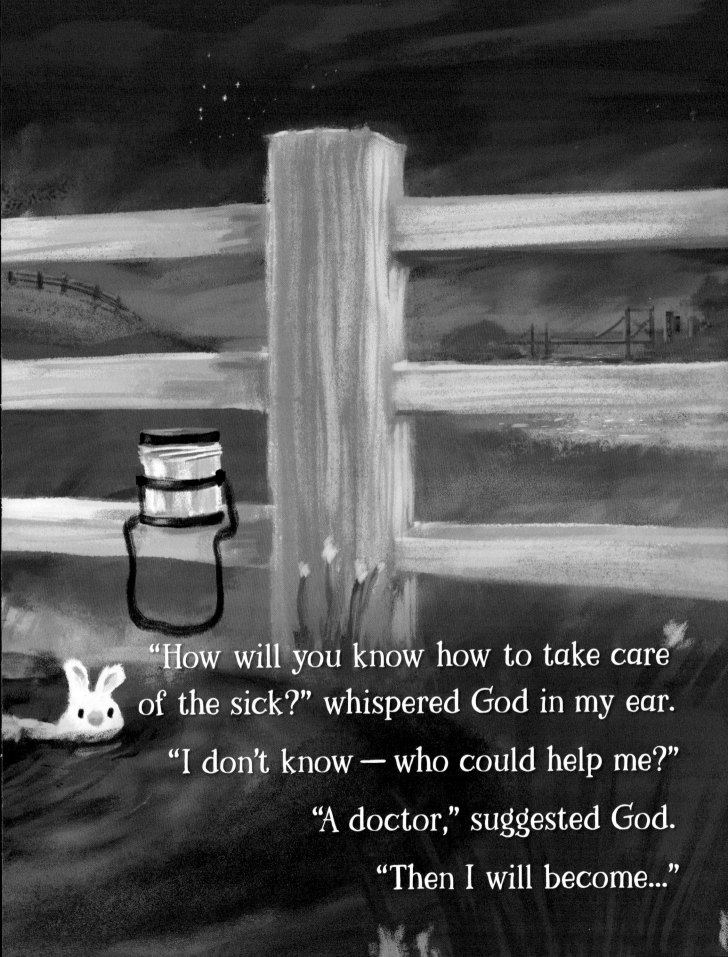

"How will you know how to take care of the sick?" whispered God in my ear.

"I don't know — who could help me?"

"A doctor," suggested God.

"Then I will become..."

A doctor!

"They are very important because they know just what to do to make everybody healthy."

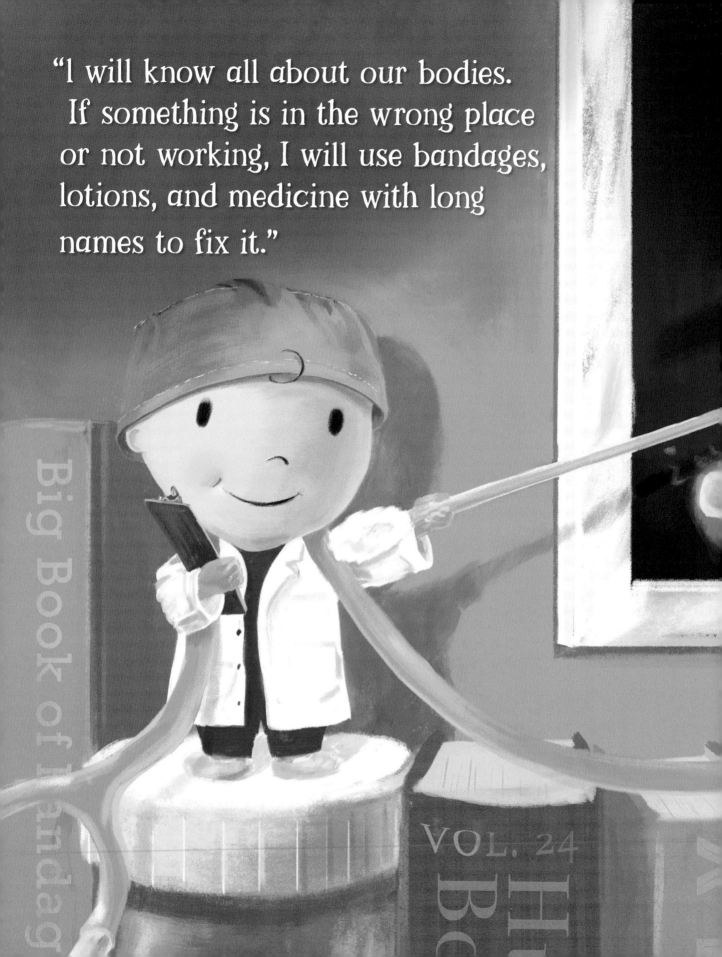

"I will know all about our bodies. If something is in the wrong place or not working, I will use bandages, lotions, and medicine with long names to fix it."

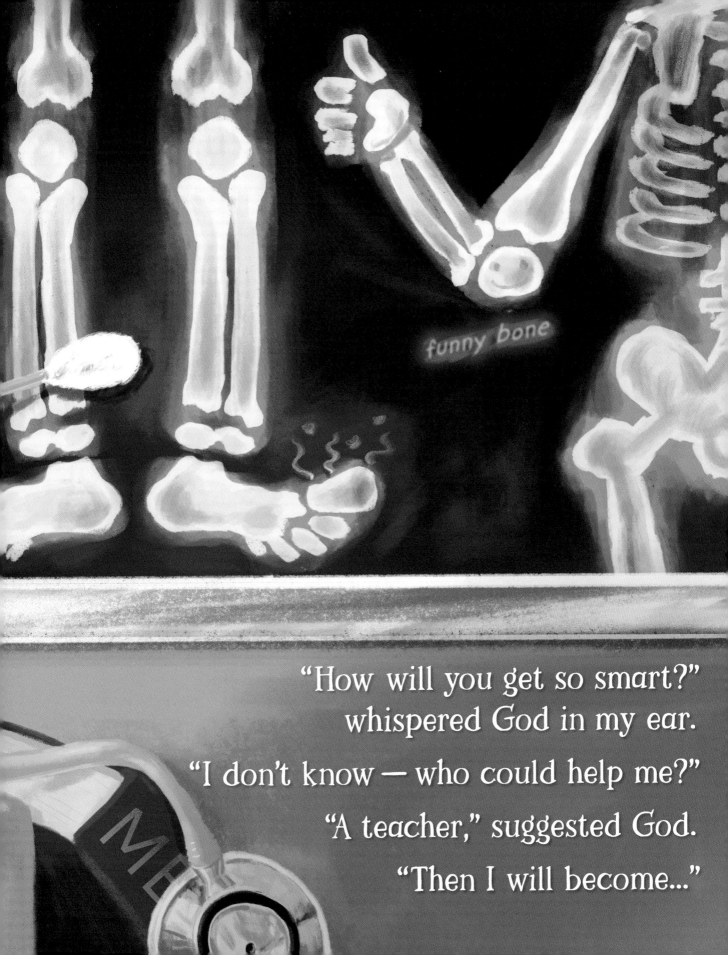

"How will you get so smart?" whispered God in my ear.

"I don't know — who could help me?"

"A teacher," suggested God.

"Then I will become..."

A teacher!

"They are very important because they help people learn new things to become the best they can be."

"I will teach everyone how to do things they never thought they could do. And if someone struggles, I will give them a hug and say, "That's OK. Let's try again".

"How will you get so patient, helpful, and kind?" whispered God in my ear.

"I don't know — who could help me?"

"Parents," suggested God.

"Then I will become..."

A parent!

"They are very important because they do the special things that make lives happy and safe."

"I will have an endless supply of hugs. I will do the right thing even when I'm grouchy. And I will help around the house—even if it's not mine!"

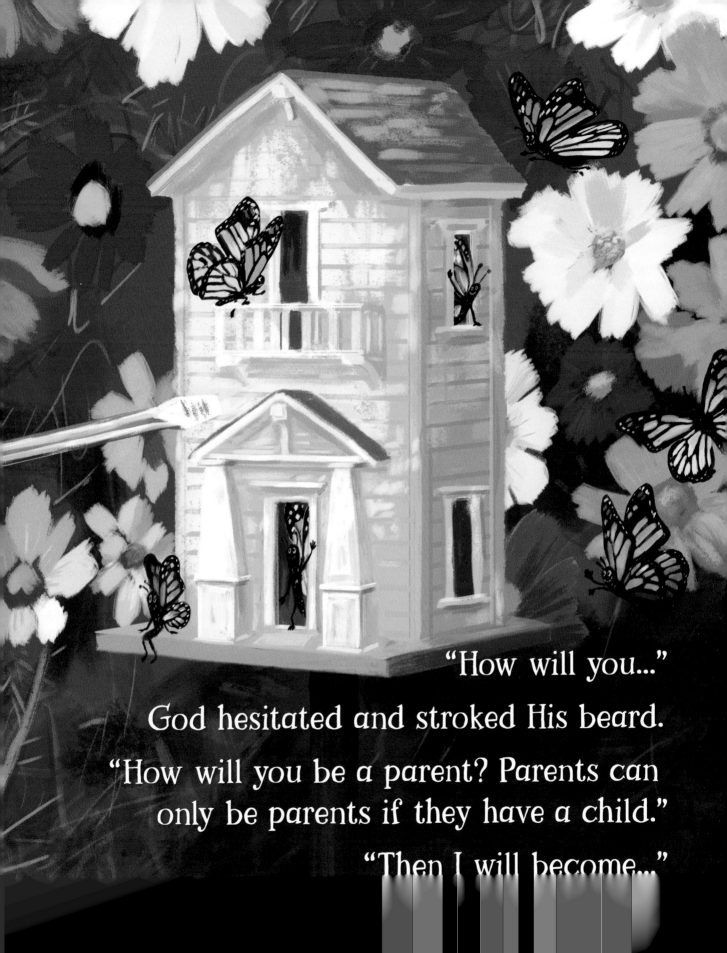

"How will you..."

God hesitated and stroked His beard.

"How will you be a parent? Parents can only be parents if they have a child."

"Then I will become..."

A child!

"They are very important because they... because... hmmm..." I shrugged and looked up at God. "What do they do?"

His eyes smiled deeply into mine. "It's not what they do; it's who they are that makes them important. You see, a child is love... My love!" beamed God.

"A child is love?! Then I definitely want to become a child! When do I start?"

God chuckled, "You've already started!
You've been a child for many months now!
And you are just a moment away from being
given to your mother and father."

God's words overwhelmed me with joy!

But, if I was with my parents,
where would He be?

God's answer came quickly.
"Don't be afraid, little one; just listen
to your heart, and you will know that
I am with you always."

I felt His warm, sweet breath, and as
He kissed me, I was born!

I'm older now, and even though I don't remember what it was like when I was with God, I remember the first thing He ever said to me, because it still echoes in my heart:

"You are a very important person whom I will always love."

The End